How To Make Money Selling Used Books on Amazon

By
Gerald Zimmerman

Copyright: © 2013 - Gerald R. Zimmerman

All Rights Reserved.
No part of this publication may be reproduced in any form or by any means, including scanning, photocopying, or otherwise without prior authorization of the copyright holder.

ISBN-13 - 978-1502308481
ISBN-10 - 1502308487

This book is published by Jershar Enterprises, through the facilities of CreateSpace.com --
An Amazon Company.

Dedication

I dedicate this book
to my wife and family,
who have put up with
so many different,
(and sometimes crazy)
ideas and schemes.

Table of Contents

Chapter 1 – How Can I Make A Living On Line? 5

Chapter 2 – The Internet Sales Machine - Amazon.com 8

Chapter 3 – Where Do I Find Books To Sell? 13

Chapter 4 – The Next Step – Get Them Ready To List! 22

Chapter 5 – Listing Your Books For Sale on Amazon.com 26

Chapter 6 – You've Made A Sale! Yippee! 32

Chapter 7 – And It Continues 35

Chapter 8 – Allow Me One Last Word, Please! 39

Chapter 1
How Can I Make A Living On Line?

If you are reading this book, then you are probably like millions of others who are looking for a good way to earn some extra money on line. Right? Of course, I'm right. That's why you are here.

I have been in exactly the same place as you. And I have scoured the web looking for just the right thing, the right combination, to help support my family and our way of life.

I started doing this before the financial downturn that we are suffering through right now. I was looking for extra money in the checkbook. And I found it in a number of places. But today, with things as they are, it is often a matter of making money to live on, rather than just extra money. And it is with that in mind that I am writing this book. I want to tell you about a possibility for you that could lead to excellent income in the future. And the good part is, you can start this with a very minimal upfront investment. But more on that later.

First though, I want to make sure that you and I are on the same page in our thinking. You see, back in the beginning, I was convinced that if I found just one good thing, it would change my life forever. And as I read the sales pages for dozens of possibilities, they all indicated that their program was the "one thing" that was needed. In fact, some claimed that I wouldn't ever need another source of income in my lifetime. I could retire right now, and bask on the sands of the Caribbean, enjoying a tall glass of lemonade (or whatever), while my computer did all the work for me, automatically.

After many attempts, I discovered the bare truth of it. To put it mildly: That Ain't Necessarily True.

I'm sure those rags to riches stories are true – for a few lucky ones. But for most people, they really don't happen that way. It takes hard work … lots of it … to be super-successful. And no one system really works to the point that it can send you on permanent vacations.

I am sure that the last paragraph will make some "guru's" upset with me, but I promised myself that in my writing, I would be honest and tell what I know. Sugar coating the truth doesn't change it, it just distorts it. And I plan to tell it as it is. I hope you will respect me for that.

But, I digress. What I was leading up to is the following. There are many ways to go when doing business on line. And doing just one of those is foolhardy. It will take multiple "streams of income" to really make you a good profit and point you in the direction of success. Picking just one is a long-shot, at best.

This book will present you with just one possibility, and it is one that I have been quite successful with. It will make you a profit, if you work it right, and you will be on your way to business success with it. I am talking about selling used books on line.

How to set it up and where to sell the books and where to get the books and how to advertise the books … that's the purpose of this book. So read on.

Chapter 2
The Internet Sales Machine– Amazon.com

There are a number of good places to sell your wares on the Internet, and every one of them will give you the possibilities of orders and profits.

But without question, Amazon.com is the #1 place to consider. And the reasons are many, and simple. First, Amazon is the leader, the #1 marketplace on the Internet today. They have 200,000,000 (that's two hundred million) credit card numbers on file. Their sales annually top any other Internet sales venue, and in fact if you look at the sales figures for #2, #3, #4, #5 and #6 and add them together, Amazon does more than the next 5 together.

Seems like a no-brainer, doesn't it? Every day, Amazon sells thousands and thousands of items to people all over the world. You can pick an item, any item, and will most likely find it in the Amazon site. And people have come to know that over the past 12 years. The delivery system is second to none with the items arriving in attractive Amazon boxes. And Amazon even has a system where you can order any item with just one click on your computer.

Of course, you may know that Amazon started by selling books. New books and old books, and it is still a huge part of their business model. And they welcome, and encourage, people like you and me to sell our books on their site. And in doing so, we can tap into their huge following and stand a very good chance of selling our product, whether books or something else.

And a really great part of it that you can list all the books you want on their site, and access their millions of daily customers without spending a red cent (with the Individual selling program on Amazon)! They don't charge you to make a listing. You just type it in, and it is there for all to see. When the book sells, Amazon takes a small percentage of the total sale, and sends you the rest. Wow.

With Amazon, you have several choices you can make as far as merchandising your books. You can have your stock of books in your home (or office), list it on Amazon.com, sell it at which time Amazon notifies you that the book has been sold and gives you the details of the sale, then package the book for shipping, make a label, put on the postage, carry it to the post office and mail it. Quite frankly, that's the way I did it. I kept my books in my office, and at one time I had over 3,000 used books in my stock. I really liked doing it this way because I had full control.

But now you can ship all of your stock to Amazon and they will warehouse it, and when one of your books sells, they package it and send it out for you (for a small charge). Having never done that myself, I guess I am a bit prejudiced against that method because it seems to take the fun out of making the sale. You really don't have a hands-on experience of making the sale. But for some people, this is the way to go. Your choice, and isn't choice great?

There are a number of other venues on line where you can list your books, and you will have some sales from that. I had my books listed on 3 or 4 different sites, and I did sell a few books from those other sites, but the bookwork involved made it more difficult, because if I sold a book on ABC book site, then I had to remember to remove it from my inventory on Amazon, and XYZ, and QRS sites as well, or I may have the situation of selling the book two times (or more!). Telling a customer that the book you advertised is not in stock is not a good way to build a loyal following.

I will give you the names and URL's for the other companies that are available in the Appendix to this book, so you can make your own decisions regarding this. I am just telling you my experience.

You will need to set up a Amazon account, although I would be surprised if you didn't already have one. If you have purchased anything, books or some other product from Amazon in the past, then you have an account. You will just need to set up a seller account, which is a very simple, and free, process. You can get all the information on how to sign up and more by visiting www.amazon.com.

Once you are signed up, you can begin your book selling business, and start selling your books. But, you ask, where do I get the books, and how do I choose them so I don't get a bunch of junk, and how do I price them, and how should I ship them (if you decide to that on your own), and how do I package them? All great questions and that is what is about to be disclosed. Nothing here is a secret, and you could do the rest of this on your own using common sense, but let me make it a little easier for you and share my experience, and then you can copy it, tweak it, and maybe have more success than I had.

Just as a personal note – As I sit here writing this, I have a picture in my mind's eye of a person, man or woman, who has recently been downsized out of a good job, or perhaps hasn't been able to locate a good job in today's economy. I see a person who is working 40 or more hours a week at a job but is not making quite enough to support his or her family. I see a family that is crying out for just a little help financially, and is willing to work to get it.

And I see my little book helping them to achieve that goal. That's exciting. But remember, I am not promising you a bazillion dollars a week and a constant vacation. Selling books on line is a big job with lots of responsibility. But it can be fun, and it can be profitable.

So, let's get on with it.

Chapter 3
Where Do I Find Books to Sell?

When I was in my peak of selling books on line, I had people ask me, "Where do you find all the books that you have in your inventory?" And that was a good question. So, let's start our quest in that location.

I started in the book selling business because my wife and I are avid readers. We love books! And over the years, we built up quite a collection of books that were to be found on shelves, on top of furniture, in boxes, in the basement, in the garage, and just about everywhere. We didn't want to throw them away, because maybe, just maybe, we would want to read them again sometime. Of course, we seldom read a book the second time, but it was a great excuse to just let them pile up.

One day, and I remember it well, my wife meekly suggested that I find a way to get rid of some of the piles of books. My first inclination in all cases is to just dump the offending item. But in this case, I decided to try to sell them. And so, I went to eBay, and listed 20 books. I discovered that eBay had a great way to list them, just by entering the ISBN number of the book, and then the program came up with a description of the book. I just chose the price I wanted to sell the book for, (and did I ever cheat myself on this one by pricing way too low! Lesson learned!)

Within a day or two, and much to our total surprise, we had sold nearly half of the books I had listed. I remember scampering around looking for packaging material and taking that first batch to the post office, where a very friendly USPS clerk explained Media

Mail to me. When those first books were officially in the mail, we were in business.

I listed several more books, and most of them sold quickly also. You will notice I said "most of them". Some books will never sell. That's a hard lesson to learn. I mistakenly thought that any book I could put my hands on would bring instant profit. But that is not the case. And I'll explain the difference between books being salable, and not-so-salable in a bit.

One thing I did notice in this time frame was that I was paying out quite a bit in charges to eBay for selling the books, but also I was paying to list the books, even if they never sold. And their listings only lasted for 3, 5 or 7 days. Then it was re-list, and pay a listing charge again. That can get expensive, especially if you are listing several hundred books, as I quickly was starting to do.

So I started looking around at other possibilities. I was convinced by this time that I was on to something that could be good for my family, but I definitely needed to tweak the idea a bit. And finding someplace that wouldn't charge me as much to sell my products was high on the list.

That's when I discovered Amazon.com. They didn't charge a listing fee. I could list as many products as I wanted to without a charge ... until I sold the item. And then it cost me about 99 cents per item paid to Amazon. (Later, as the business grew, I joined their Professional Selling Program, and that does have a monthly cost, but no per item sold charge (unless you use their fulfillment program). That sounded a lot better to me, and I quickly moved all of my items to Amazon, and started selling.

A note of advice: There are always nay-Sayers in anything you do. Some people wouldn't be happy if everything was free, and you didn't have to do any work at all. I say this because if you read some of the blogs and chat rooms, you will find people who think that Amazon is not a good company, that they don't really look out for the little seller, and that you'll do better . . . maybe buying their special system (for only $xx.xx). I am personally sick and tired of those kind of advertisements. They usually only make the nay-sayer money, and never really make YOU any money. My personal rule is to stick with the successful (Amazon, for instance). I pass that advice on to you! (And by the way, I don't make anything for saying that. It is just my personal opinion .. free of charge!)

My sales were always good. I sold a good product (books), listed them honestly and with total disclosure (I told people if there was a scratch on the cover, or a torn page), and priced the item appropriately. In 4 years of selling books, I only had one returned to me, and that was because the book "wasn't what they were looking for" (Huh?).

OK. Back to the question at hand, "Where do I get the books to sell?" First, obviously, is from your own personal collection.

Then start looking at your family, sisters and brothers, parents, next door neighbors, and tell them you are looking for used books. You'll take them off their hands, and they can help you by letting you have them for free. Most good friends and family will gladly help you out this way. If you can get some books free, then your sales will be nearly 100% profit (only your fees to pay), and you will be on your way.

When you get free books, just take them, no matter what their condition or title. I remember getting books that had been in a flood, and the pages wouldn't even separate from each other. I got books that were missing their cover, or had whole sections of pages missing. I smiled and accepted the offer, and then disposed of those particular books. But in every case, I got books that we were able to list and sell. Thank you very much!

Next, you can start looking externally for books. This is where you will start paying for the books that you are going to have in your library. And if you are going to pay, then you need to be very careful about what you buy. To do this, you can start with your smart-phone, and pull up … you guessed it … Amazon.com. In the search box, type in the name of the book … and for our example, I typed in "Moby Dick".

The Amazon sales page will come up on your screen, and you will notice that Amazon sells it for $15.88, but that's a new book. Just under that price, you'll see "More Buying Choices – Paperback". Here you'll find listed New – from $14.00. These are books being sold by people just like you. They are listing their books on Amazon, and they have some new ones that someone will sell for $14.00. But clicking on that, you'll find that the prices for the 4 that are available in the new classification are from $14.00 to $16.00. Under that, you'll see "Used", with "from $4.25" and a notation that there are 13 available. When you click on the 'used', you see the 13 listed from $4.25 to $12.95, and the condition listed for each book. (There is also a classification for "collectible", but be careful of this one. It had better be in collectible condition, and probably signed by the author.)

You will need to determine the condition of the book at this point to really get an idea of its value. Be careful that you don't over-estimate the condition of the book. You need to get it right, because you are being looked at by the customer (and by Amazon) as being an expert. And experts don't mess around with something as important as condition. With that said, here are the guidelines.

It would be good to memorize this, or keep a copy of it on you when you are looking for books, especially in the beginning.
- New: Just as it sounds. A brand new, unused, unopened item in its original packaging.
- Used – Like New: An apparently untouched book in perfect condition. Original protective wrapping may be missing, but there are absolutely no signs of wear on the item or its cover. Item is suitable for presenting as a gift.
- Used – Very Good: A well cared-for item that has seen limited use but remains in great condition. The item is complete, unmarked, and undamaged, but may show some limited signs of wear.
- Used – Good: This item shows wear from consistent use, but remains in good condition and is complete. It may be marked, have a name written on the flyleaf, maybe limited underlining or notations on pages, but otherwise is in "good" condition.
- Used – Acceptable: This item is fairly worn but continues to be usable. Signs of wear can include aesthetic issues such as scratches, dents, and worn coves. The item may have identifying markings on it or show other signs of previous use.

Believe me when I tell you that this is very, very important. Your future business depends on it.

By the way, after you are under way, you can purchase a PDA, or a scanner to go on your smart phone that will automatically look up the book and tell you the price range. You'll see people using them at some of the places where you go, and when you can afford one, you need to get one. But don't rush it. You can do it the long way as described above until you are under way. In other words, don't spend your profits before you have profits to spend!

Now you have an idea of what the book sells for. At $4.25 you can make a good profit, if you buy it at the right price. So, buy it. And maybe yours will be in a condition that will get $6 or $7 for you.

Do this with each book you find. It won't guarantee sales, but at least you'll know if someone is selling the very same book at only a penny or two. You can't compete with that!

Where to look for those books? My favorite place (among others) was at Thrift Stores. In fact, my best finds were at Goodwill and Salvation Army thrift stores, although I did find some at the local, privately owned stores. Just go in, find the book section, and start at one end and go to the other. There is a major Salvation Army store in my location that has thousands upon thousands of books to look through. I usually spent the better part of a day at that store every few weeks. I chose the category of book I was searching for carefully, and then went through everything.

The inclination here will be to see a "pretty" cover, and decide it looks so good that it will certainly sell, and then find out it is only worth a few cents. Don't buy it if you don't research it.

Check with your local library to find out if they hold an annual book sale. Most of them do, and they can be a goldmine for you. But be prepared for lots of competition. It is here that you will probably want to have your PDA or scanner ready to go. I remember going to my first Library Sale, and some guy just pushed right past me as he scanned book after book, 8-10 a minute, and took what he wanted. There was no way I could keep up with him. At the next Library Sale I went to, it was me rushing down the aisles with my PDA unit.

Another source would be yard or garage sales. Quite frankly, I was never real successful at these, but I did stop at some of them in the more affluent neighborhoods.

Estate sales can be a wonderful source of finding books. Again, go prepared and quietly look up the books, either on your smart-phone or PDA unit. And then you'll need to haggle on the price, as sometimes they are way overpriced at the estate sale. Don't buy something that you can't make a profit on. That just makes good sense.

Watch the local paper want-ads for book sales at churches, schools and other public places. You never know what you may find.

This is a partial, but good list of places to look for books. Actually, in my search for books, these are the main places I looked. And I kept track of where I went each time, and what the results of my search were. A notebook with a page for each location works, or you can do a spreadsheet on your computer, but keep track.

True story: I had a very favorite place to go and look for books, not necessarily because they always had a good stock of books (which they did), but because I became friends with the people who worked at that thrift store. We would visit, and laugh and carry on, and I might even find a few books. Sometimes they would hold books in the back room and let me go through them before they put them out for the general public (and other sellers). But I visited there way too often, and that reduced my effectiveness in looking for books.

At the larger thrift stores, ask what day they usually get books in from their sorting facilities. Goodwill and Salvation Army have main locations where items are sorted and divided between their several stores. And there is usually a specific day of the week when they deliver those books to the store. I remember that Tuesday was the day at my favorite store, and they usually came before 10 in the morning. I made sure I was there by 9:30 so I could be first to see the new books. You've gotta be on your toes and looking for the best opportunities, all the time!

As to what price you should pay for a book, that is your choice. I had an absolute top price that I would buy a book for ... let's just say it was $4. Unless it was an extremely hard to find title or book, I didn't pay more than my maximum. And I seldom did. Most of the times when I eased up on my rule, it came back to bite me in the end. I've said it before, and so it is again: You gotta make a profit.

Doing this will bring you a goodly number of books. Keep all your receipts when you purchase the books (tax deductions!) and bring them home.

Now the real fun begins :-)

Chapter 4
The Next Step –
Get Them Ready To List

Do you remember when you were a child and what you felt like on Christmas morning when you saw all the gifts under the tree? Brings a smile to your face, doesn't it. Well, that's what I felt like every week when I got home with my bags of books from my buying trip.

Sometimes, it would be 30 or 40 books, and once in a while it might be over 100 books from my buying spree. But whatever, it was exciting to see them come out of the bags and put into piles, usually on the living room floor. Now before you get too excited and start taking them out of their bags, here is a suggestion:

If you know that you spent about $2.50 each for the books you bought at the ABC Thrift store, then as you take those books out of the bag, write the cost on a post-it note (I used the 2x2 inch ones) and stick it to the cover of the book. You'll add more to that slip later.

Now stack them on the floor or table or where ever. On my post-it, I even devised a code for each specific location where I bought books. For instance, if I bought it at Goodwill on First Street, I wrote "G-1" on the post-it, and then the price paid. I like as much information as possible, so it worked for me. That way, if there was a question about the books price, it would help me remember the buying atmosphere.

The stacks I put the books in were by condition of the book (see the chart above). The place you put them now can be changed as you look more carefully at the book, but at least you're starting out right.

Now start on a pile, and on your computer, go to Amazon.com, and do the whole look-up thing again, and find the price range for used books of that title. Write the range on your post-it. For instance, the used books run from 4.25 – 12.95. So write "U=4.25-12.95(13)". Now you have a reference point of what this book sells for and how many are on Amazon. Now look carefully at the book, open it, and look for markings, names, pencil marks, underlining, torn pages, turned page corners, damage to the book spine, the condition of the books dust-cover (if it has one), and determine where you are going to put it for condition: Used-Like New (LN); Used-Very Good (VG); Used-Good (G); Used-Acceptable (A).

Do this to every book. If you find a book that isn't what you want to sell for some reason, perhaps missing pages, or too much writing in the book, or someone spilled a bottle of strawberry jelly on the pages!!!, or some other reason, then get rid of it. You are only going to sell books that you can be proud of, and would want on your bookshelf at your home. Believe me, your reputation as a bookseller is very important to future sales.

Now that you've sorted them out, and given them a condition rating, it is time to start the really hard part of the whole equation. You need to price them and list them.

Pricing is a subjective thing, and you will need to develop your own method. But let me give you a few guidelines that I developed for my business.

First, you need to understand who your customers are. That is the case in any business, whether a clothing store, a restaurant, or a bookstore. You need to understand that people who are searching for a used book on line are looking for the best price possible. If they want a new book, they will be willing to pay the high price. But used books sell for less than high. So, you need to take that into consideration.

Going back to our "Moby Dick" book that we bought for $2, but sells used for $4.25 – $12.95, we must look first at the condition. I see we have it listed as "Used-Good", and the reason is because there is a name written on the inside of the front cover, and quite a number of page corners are turned over, which was the former owners way of keeping track of where he left off. If I go back to the Amazon listing of used, I will find that books in the "good" condition are listed at $4.25 – $5.50. I will want to stay in that range, and will probably list close to the bottom, or $4.25 – 4.75 in price. (My own practice would have been to price it at $4.28 to stay close to the lowest price. I like odd sales price numbers!)

A temptation would be to list it for $4.00 and be the lowest, but you can always lower the price if it doesn't sell within 30-60 days. But don't short-change yourself at this point. Get as much as you can for it.

So, again you will write your retail price on the post-it (R=4.28), and move it to the "ready" pile. After you've gone through the whole lot of books you purchased, now you are ready to list them on Amazon.

Chapter 5
Listing Your Books For Sale
(on Amazon, of course)

I mentioned earlier that there are a number of sites where you can list your books for sale. But for our purposes here, I will focus in on listing on Amazon, because that is where a majority of your sales will come from. Once you learn to do this right, you can easily figure out the other sites.

Here is a kind of stupid thing I discovered. When I got to my desk to start listing the books, I never put more than 5 books on the desk at a time. Early on, I put over 50 books on my desk, and I spent the whole time worried about that high pile and how I would ever get done with it all. But putting just 5 books there made me think that I was doing well, and somehow made the job easier. Like I said, it is kind of stupid, but it worked for me.

When you list books, PLEASE be accurate and professional. Don't hurry to get it done at the expense of making your customer think you don't know what you are doing. That would be like going into a clothing store, and the clerk bringing out a dress size 24 when you are a size 6. You'd know right then that he doesn't have a clue. Well, listing your books online is the same thing. In this case though, make sure you don't make typing errors, or misspelled words, or all lower case letters, or all upper case letters. Do it right the first time. Proof-read everything you type. And then proof it again before you hit ENTER. Be professional. If you have problems with this, then find someone who will help you. I'm serious. You are in business now, so do what you would expect a store-owner to do in your presence.

All right, go to Amazon.com, and get to the Sellers Area. You signed up to be a seller, whether Individual or Professional, and they sent you an email that explained what to do to enter a product. So get to that point.

Books have an interesting number on them. If you have the dust cover, or if you are working with a paperback book, look at the back of the book, usually just above the bar-code. You'll find a number listed – either 10 or 13 numbers long (they have been changing all of them over the past few years and the newer books have 13 digit numbers). In the case of our "Moby Dick" book, the number you would find is 978-1613823101. This is the ISBN number, or International Standard Book Number. Every book that has been published in the last 75 years or so has one of these numbers, and it identifies it and separates it out from every other book published.

In the Amazon Sellers area, you enter that ISBN number without any hyphens or other punctuation, and wonderful things happen. Up will pop the Moby Dick description, and most of the time, a picture of the cover of the book. If it's the right book and the right cover, then click the button to the right that says, "Sell Yours".

This will bring up the Product Summary and sales page. Now just go down the list and enter the information. OK. I'll go to each item with you, and again our example will be our favorite, Moby Dick.

- First notice that at the top there is a picture of your cover, as well as an ASIN number which is an Amazon generated number for this title. Also, you'll see competing Marketplace offers, which is much of the same information that we looked up earlier. The Amazon list price of $15.88, and the sales rank of 51,792. (These numbers are as of the moment that I am looking at this page, but these numbers change constantly, so it may be different when you see it.) The Amazon Sales Ranking is the indication of what position this book is in sales wise, or how often does it sell. A number over 5,000 is probably a month or more to sell the book. Obviously, the lower the number, the faster the book of this title will sell.

- **Seller SKU**: This is like an inventory number. Perhaps you have all your books numbered on the shelf. In that case, what is the number you've assigned to this book?. In our example, it is located on the 5th shelving unit, and is book #1078. So in the Seller SKU it could be 05-1078. You don't need to fill this out if you don't want to, but as you grow, you will need an inventory system to keep track of where the books are.
- **Condition**. Right away, we're into the important stuff. The pull-down reveals those condition classes we talked about earlier. Just click the one you chose. We'll say our book is "Very Good".
- **Condition Note**: Always fill this out. Why did you pick "Very Good"? Maybe you'll write: "This book is in very good condition with no damage to the spine, no markings evident in the book, no damage to the covers". In the case of a hardbound book, if it has a dust cover, tell what the condition of that is.

- **Low Price**: When you selected "Very Good", Amazon provided you with the lowest price this book is being offered for on Amazon. In this case, it's $4.25 (plus shipping). You have the option to either match the low price, or go on from here.
- **Your Price**: Here, you enter the price you've decided on that you will sell the book for. In our case, we'll put in $4.28.
- **Sale Price**: I never used this, but let's say the book has a value of $15.00, but for the first 5 days you'd sell it at the reduced price of $10.00. Put that price here, and enter the start and ending date for the sale.
- **Quantity**: Self-evident, if you have 3 copies of this book, you put "3" here. The system will keep track of your inventory, and reduce the number as you sell the copies.
- **Start Selling Date**: Put in today's date. If you don't want to sell this book until next Tuesday, then put that date in.
- **Restock Date**: You probably won't use this, but if you have a book that you have ordered to replace what you have already sold, and you know it is coming in on the 4th, then put that date in, and Amazon will list the book on that day.
- **Country of publication**: Look on the publishers page in the book and check where the book was published (what country)
- **Import designation**: Probably won't use this, but the instructions are right there.
- **Country as labeled**: Complete this ONLY if import designation (#12) is imported.

The next section on this page has to do with how you will ship the book to the buyer, and what the cost will be that the customer will pay.

Most of the time I chose "Standard Shipping", which includes using Media Mail. The customer normally receives their package in 3-9 days, and it costs you less for the postage. The other choice that you can add to Standard is Expedited which would be USPS Priority Mail.

In the shipping area, you will see the price you listed for your book, the shipping credit which is charged to the customer, the amount of the commission that Amazon keeps, and the amount that will be transferred to your checking account. From that amount, you deduct the amount you will pay the post office to mail your package, and now you've got your bottom line profit.

The information we just entered is enough to get your product listed in the Amazon catalog, and begin your selling career on Amazon. Do this for each book, being careful to be professional and honest on every question, and you're on your way to success.

Chapter 6
You've Made A Sale! Yippee!

Check your email regularly. Because all of a sudden, without notice or fanfare, you're going to get an email from Amazon.com that says that you have made a sale. It will give you information about the sale, and give you instructions of what to do to get the rest of the information. This changes every once in a while, so I'll just leave it that you should follow the instructions in the email.

But what you will do is get the book ready to ship.

You'll need a few supplies for this. After you've been in business for a while, and are getting lots of orders, you can buy these things in bulk, but to start with, go to WalMart and purchase a package or two of Padded Envelopes, size #4, which are about 11x14 inches. This will work for almost every book you will have to sell, unless you have some of the "coffee table" over-sized books. Then, you will need to find something that will fit those.

Use the padded envelopes, as it will prevent injury to the books during shipping.

I also added an extra feature to the shipping of my books. I wrapped the book in a gallon size food bag, like a Hefty or Glad brand Storage bag. Or, you can wrap the book in a plastic wrap like Saran Wrap, for instance. These will keep the book dry and safe during shipment. I did the little extra, and it was mentioned many times in feedback notes. You don't have to do it, but I thought it was a good idea.

Now, join Stamps.com, or one of the on line systems to be able to print out the label with the postage already paid. I personally liked the service provided by PayPal, and it worked out really good. I purchased some special label paper that you peel and stick, with the size of the label being about ½ the size of a piece of typing paper.

When you print out your label, choose "Media Mail" from the listing on Stamps.com, or PayPal, or whatever service you are using. It costs less, and I found that the delivery times were very good.

Get a tape dispenser that takes 2" wide tape, like they use to tape boxes in a warehouse, and a supply of tape. (You can always print the labels on plain paper, and then tape them down onto the package if you don't have the sticky ones).

After wrapping the book in plastic wrap or a food bag, and placing it in the padded envelope, and sealing the envelope, old careful, over protective ME used some of the 2" tape to make sure the padded envelope stayed closed. Then apply the label, and take it to the post office and drop it off. (By the way, if the package is over 14 ounces, you need to take the package into the post office, and not drop it in a mailbox somewhere. Since terrorism and bombings have become a part of daily life in this world, they don't want heavier things in the mail boxes.)

Hey! Guess what. You are now really in business. You've made your first sale. You've packaged your book for shipping. You've applied the label. And, you've mailed the package to the lucky customer. Congratulations!

Chapter 7
And It Continues . . .

It's exciting, isn't it? And it will be even more exciting when you see that first customer give you a positive feedback on your Amazon account.

Now, you just continue to do what you've learned how to do. Go out and find books, from wherever you can find them. Carefully choose the ones that you want to sell. Maybe even start specializing in a certain genre of books, like cookbooks (which don't really sell all that well), or westerns, or terror, or romance. Maybe you just want to handle non-fiction, although fiction sells better. It's your business, and you can do whatever you want!

Grade the condition of your books carefully and honestly. If it isn't all that great, say so. The customer will know what they are going to get if they buy, and believe me, they will buy it.

Price the book at a price that will make you a profit, but not be overpriced in the marketplace making it impossible to sell. Be smart in this area.

Keep your shelves and inventory listings up-to-date.

Be proud of your business. If, after you list a book, you happen to look at the listing and see that you misspelled the name of the book, change it. If you need to change the price you are charging for the book, change it, but do so carefully so you don't make a wrong decision.

Keep careful records of everything you buy, and everything you sell. Keep records of where you drive to buy books, giving starting and ending mileage for the trip, and where you went and how many books you bought that day. This is for Tax Purposes. We don't like to think about that, but you will have to list the sales of the books as income on April 15th.

Become active in the activities of your local public library system. Let them know who you are and what you are doing. You might be surprised at their reaction and help if you need it. And they may let you know if they have some duplicate books they need to get rid of.

Make professional contacts with organizations of booksellers. Google to find these organizations, and get on their mailing list.

Get some business cards printed (VistaPrint.com is a great place as their prices are very low). Give your card to people who might have some books to sell in the future that you can pick up at a good price. Let people know who you are and what you are doing.

Don't spend money that you can't afford to spend. There were times when I only had $20 to spend when I went to buy books. I bought carefully, but did not go over my limit. The next time I went I had more, and bought more. Don't go into debt buying books. It is better to have 20 books listed that you actually own, than 100 books listed that you owe money for. Remember, some, or even most of the books you buy may not sell for a long time. Be careful with your money.

Give back to the community. Whether it is through charitable gifts to schools or day care centers. (They love to get children's books in good condition for their library. And if you can't sell them easily, why not donate a few of them. You'll be a champion for doing it).

Be honest. Hold your head up high and be proud of what you are doing. In selling books, you are contributing to the learning experience of the customer, as well as providing hours and hours of entertainment while they read the books that you have made available to them.

And finally, be a proud bookseller. And I wish you the very best in your new venture, Mr or Ms Bookseller!

Chapter 8
Allow Me One Last Word, Please!

Allow me to bring up one more thing before I go. And I'll do it in a hurry – just a few words.

I have always wanted to write a book. You know, I've wanted to be a published author. And it took until I was in my 60's to accomplish the dream. You have just read that first book!

I am very proud of this book. I started by listing this book on Kindle, which is an Amazon company. You can write a book, list it for free (my favorite word) on Amazon Kindle, and make up to 70% of the selling price every time one sells.

No publisher. No agent. No waiting for approvals or jumping through endless, and sometimes expensive hoops. Just write, publish, and enjoy the beneifts.

Now, I am moving on to a new venue. I am publishing this book as a paperb ack – the kind that you can hold in your hand, rather than the electronic kind of e-book, or in my case, a Kindle. Nothing wrong with e-books. I love them. But some people still don't have a Kindle or any of the other brands that are out there.

So publishing a paper back is a big thing.

And again, it is Amazon who comes to the rescue by offering a service that you can use . . . and again, it's free. What you are holding in your hand right now is an example of that.

I am not going to give all the details here. Maybe it will be a new book later on. But, you can go to: **https://createspace.com,** and you will find all the details and lots of information about how to do it.

I also learned a great deal from watching some YouTube videos on the subject.

As I said, I may write a book about my experience of publishing this book on Create Space after a short time passes, but for now, just know that this is an availability that is open to you, too.

Maybe there is a book floating around in the gray matter of your brain that people will want, buy, and enjoy in the future. Kindle and Create Space can make it a reality for you, just like it did for me.

Acknowledgements

I would like to thank the people who have helped me in this project.

Of course, first and foremost, I thank my Lord and Savior, Jesus Christ, for giving me the patience, the knowledge, and the abilities that are required. Without Him, life would be totally meaningless.

I also want to thank my wife, Sharon. She is the reason I do the things that I do everyday. Although time has taken its toll on her ability to do things and to get around, she remains steadfast in her faith, and in her love for me. It is hard to believe that we have been married for 50 years now, and every bit of it has been a joy.

My children, Tammy, Scott and Cherry are always helpful and encouraging.

And my grandchildren. All 5 of them. They are the reason for life and living these days. I love to joke that I don't know why we didn't just start with grandchildren. They are wonderful.

And finally, to you the reader. I wrote this book because I feel what you are feeling. I needed an outlet for my frustrations, and selling things online, like books and so much more, gave me that outlet. It has also provided enough money to improve our daily lives.

May God bless you richly as you continue in your quest for a better life.

                                        Gerald Zimmerman.

                                        jz1304@gmail.com

Made in the USA
Monee, IL
06 August 2021